READING RESOURCE
CORONADO HILLS ELE

MW00887155

VOICES FROM THE CIVIL WAR

by Susan Brocker

Table of Contents

A House Divided

> *A house divided against itself cannot stand.*
> *I believe this government cannot endure*
> *permanently half slave and half free.*
>
> Abraham Lincoln, 1858

Between 1861 and 1865, Americans fought a war that split their nation in two and changed it forever. Men who had once been friends faced each other across the battlefield. In some families brother fought against brother, father against son. More Americans lost their lives in this war than in any other war.

The Civil War was a conflict between the northern states and the southern states. It had many causes. One was the different economies and ways of life of the North and the South. Another was the disagreements between the southern states and the federal government over their rights and powers. But the main cause was the issue of slavery.

The cities of the North were major industrial areas. Many were also centers of trade.

The South had a rural way of life and an agricultural economy that depended on slave labor. In contrast, the North's economy was based on trade and industry. Its factories and cities were growing.

By the early 1800s, many northern voices were raised against slavery. **Abolitionists** (ab-uh-LIHSH-uhn-ihsts) called for slavery to be outlawed.

But Southerners opposed the end of slavery. To further complicate things, new territories and states, formed from the settlement of the West, wanted to join the Union. People argued over whether these new states should allow slavery.

In 1820 the first of two compromises was reached. The Missouri Compromise admitted Missouri to the Union as a slave state and Maine as a free state. It also banned slavery in new states north of 36°30' N latitude.

Cotton plantations, part of the South's agricultural economy, were worked by slaves who had no rights or freedoms. They were bought and sold as property.

The Compromise of 1850 admitted California as a free state. It also introduced the idea of **popular sovereignty** (SAHV-ren-tee): citizens of each territory should decide whether to be a free or slave state.

The Fugitive Slave Law was also passed in 1850. It required escaped slaves captured in the North to be returned to their owners. This law did not give fugitives, or people who had fled from danger, any legal rights. As a result, many legally freed slaves were taken south and sold as slaves.

At about this time, Harriet Beecher Stowe wrote *Uncle Tom's Cabin*. Both the book and the Fugitive Slave Law helped work up antislavery feeling.

In 1854 Congress passed the Kansas-Nebraska Act. It made popular sovereignty the law. Fighting between abolitionists and pro-slavery forces followed.

Point

Read More About It

Using resource materials, read more about *Uncle Tom's Cabin* to determine the political implications of this book.

Uncle Tom's Cabin, by Harriet Beecher Stowe, told the tale of a kindly slave beaten to death by a cruel owner.

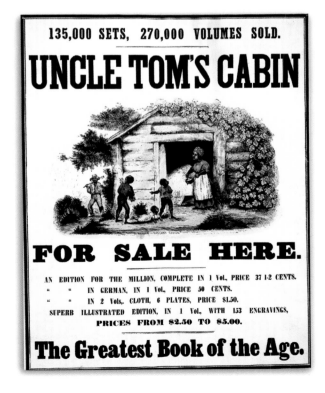

135,000 SETS, 270,000 VOLUMES SOLD.

UNCLE TOM'S CABIN

FOR SALE HERE.

AN EDITION FOR THE MILLION, COMPLETE IN 1 Vol., PRICE 37 1-2 CENTS.
"   "   IN GERMAN, IN 1 Vol., PRICE 50 CENTS.
"   "   IN 2 Vols., CLOTH, 6 PLATES, PRICE $1.50.
SUPERB ILLUSTRATED EDITION, IN 1 Vol., WITH 153 ENGRAVINGS,
PRICES FROM $2.50 TO $5.00.

The Greatest Book of the Age.

The Dred Scott Decision further divided the nation. Dred Scott was a slave who sued for his freedom because he had once lived in a free state. The Supreme Court ruled that slaves could not be citizens. In 1859 the famous abolitionist John Brown tried to start a slave revolt. He was tried and hanged for treason for taking over the arsenal at Harper's Ferry, West Virginia.

In 1860, the Republican candidate Abraham Lincoln was elected president. Southerners feared that he would try to abolish slavery. Some southern states decided to **secede** (suh-SEED) from the Union. They believed that individual states had rights that the federal government could not take away. South Carolina was the first state to secede, followed by Mississippi, Alabama, Florida, Georgia, Louisiana, and Texas. On February 4, 1861, these seven rebel states formed the Confederate States of America. They elected Jefferson Davis as president.

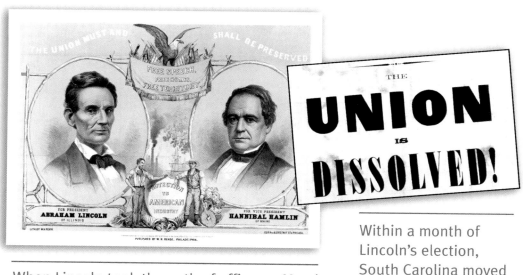

When Lincoln took the oath of office on March 4, 1861, he told the nation that he had a duty to preserve, protect, and defend the Union.

Within a month of Lincoln's election, South Carolina moved the nation toward war.

Although President Lincoln was against the spread of slavery into new states, he tried to reassure the South that he would not abolish slavery in any of the existing slave states. But he firmly believed that no state had the right to secede from the Union.

On April 12, 1861, the newly formed Confederate army fired on Fort Sumter, South Carolina. Lincoln called for volunteers to fight for the fort. The South saw this as an act of war. Four more states left the Union. The war between the North and South had begun.

This map shows the division of the states on the eve of war. Eleven slave states made up the Confederate States of America. Four slave states, 19 free states, and several territories fought for the Union.

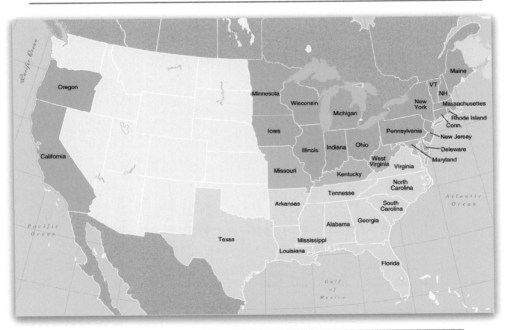

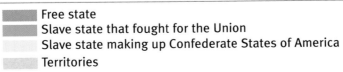

Free state
Slave state that fought for the Union
Slave state making up Confederate States of America
Territories

Thousands of men from both sides rushed to volunteer as soldiers. They were eager to fight for their home states.

The Union soldiers wore uniforms of blue. The Confederate soldiers wore uniforms of gray. Both sides were certain of victory in what they thought would be a brief war.

But this war was to be like no other. Long and terrible, it would touch everyone and shape the nation's future.

In the following chapters, you will read about many events of the Civil War. You will also "hear from" people who were involved in the events firsthand.

In the words of a Confederate soldier,

At every town and station, citizens and ladies were waving their handkerchiefs and hurrahing for Jeff Davis and the Southern Confederacy... Ah, it is worth soldiering to receive such welcomes as this.

In towns and cities in the North and South, young men anxious to be soldiers for their cause hurried to sign up as volunteers.

CHAPTER 2

Voices from the Battlefield

*E*ach side went to war sure it would be the winner. The North had more people and money than the South. It had more factories to make guns and military supplies. But the South had a fighting spirit. The Confederate soldiers were fine horsemen and marksmen. Many of their leaders had been educated at military schools, including West Point.

The first major battle of the war was the Battle of Bull Run, fought along a stream near Manassas, Virginia. Fighting was furious. Southern reinforcements and the leadership of General T. J. Jackson, later known as "Stonewall" Jackson, finally gave victory to the South. The Union forces broke and ran.

Point

Read More About It

Stonewall Jackson did not live to see the end of the Civil War. Using resource materials, read more to find out what happened to him.

Union troops clashed with Confederate soldiers at the Battle of Bull Run.

The battle left wounded and dead soldiers everywhere. People now realized that the war would not be won in a single battle.

Over the next four years, the terrible scene would be repeated again and again. There would be more and more wounded and dead.

A Confederate soldier at the Battle of Bull Run later wrote,

For ten long hours it literally rained balls, shells and other missiles of destruction...The sight of the dead, the cries of the wounded, the thundering noise of battle can never be put on paper. The dead, the dying and the wounded, all mixed up together, friend and foe embraced in death...

Union soldiers posed in front of their artillery reinforcements.

After Bull Run, both sides realized that trained armies would be needed to win the war. Few soldiers had any military experience. Most were farmers or laborers. Many were little more than boys. To teach them how to march and handle weapons, army camps were started.

As a Union soldier at army camp wrote to his family,

The first thing in the morning is drill. Then drill, then drill again. Then drill, drill, a little more drill. The drill, and lastly drill. Between drills, we drill, and sometimes stop to eat a little and have roll call.

With varying amounts of training, soldiers were sent to the battlefields. Between battles, the soldiers carried out chores, cleaned weapons, and sewed torn uniforms. They traded books and newspapers, kept diaries, and wrote letters home.

Music was important to army life, and not only as a form of entertainment. Soldiers marched to the **fife** and drum. They woke up and went to sleep to the buglers' sounds. They went into battle and moved on the battlefield according to the buglers' music. Many musicians were young. A famous Union drummer boy was Johnny Clem. He went to war when he was only nine.

At night, soldiers sat around their campfires, singing songs about home. Going into battle, they sang stirring marches. A Confederate favorite was *Dixie*, while Union troops marched to *The Battle Cry of Freedom*.

Popular Civil War songs were written to arouse patriotic feelings. Soldiers sang and played harmonicas and banjos.

At the Battle of Shiloh, Johnny Clem's drum was destroyed by enemy fire. This gave him the nickname "Johnny Shiloh."

Hundreds of reporters, artists, and photographers traveled with the armies. For the first time, reports were sent immediately from the battlefield by telegraph. The public could read about battles the next day, instead of weeks later.

Artists, such as Alfred Waud, sketched battle scenes as they happened. The work was dangerous and the artists were often fired upon.

Photographers carried their heavy cameras into battle in order to capture the horrors of war. After the bloody Battle of Antietam (an-TEET-uhm), photographers led by Mathew Brady took the first photos of fallen soldiers.

Mathew Brady's photos, for which he became famous, brought the horrors of war home to those not engaged on the battlefields.

The Battle of Antietam was the bloodiest day of the war. General Robert E. Lee led his Confederate troops into Union territory. On September 17, 1862, the two armies met near the village of Sharpsburg, Maryland. The battle raged all day. When night fell, about 2,000 Union soldiers and 2,700 Confederate soldiers lay dead. Lee withdrew.

Lincoln declared the battle a Union victory. He told the Confederate states that if they did not return to the Union by January 1, 1863, their slaves would be freed. The war that had begun as a struggle to save the Union had also become a fight to end slavery.

A 16-year-old soldier at the battle of Antietam later wrote to his father,

We rushed onto them every man for himself–all loading and firing as fast as he could see a rebel to shoot at. The firing increased tenfold until it sounded like the rolls of thunder–and all the time every man shouting as loud as he could.

In this photograph, bodies awaited burial in a field at Antietam, Maryland.

Many brave nurses and doctors worked on the battlefields. They set up temporary hospitals and tended to the wounded. Clara Barton, who later founded the American Red Cross, nursed the wounded at Antietam. Often there were not enough doctors, nurses, or medical supplies to treat all the sick and wounded. Many more soldiers died from wounds or disease than died in battle.

A Confederate nurse wrote in her diary,

I sat up all night, bathing the men's wounds, and giving them water. Every one attending to them seemed completely worn out. Some of the doctors told me that they had scarcely slept since the battle...The men are lying all over the house, on their blankets, just as they were brought from the battlefield.

An artist's rendering of women volunteers at work in a Union hospital.

The war's turning point came on July 1, 1863, when General Lee again invaded Union territory. Union troops led by General George Gordon Meade met Lee in the town of Gettysburg, Pennsylvania.

For two days the battle raged on without a clear winner. On the third day, General Lee ordered an attack on the center of the Union line. About 13,000 Confederate soldiers, led by General George Pickett, marched in line nearly a mile across an open field.

Most of the men in Pickett's charge were killed or wounded. The defeat forced Lee to retreat. The Confederacy never really recovered.

Later, Abraham Lincoln visited Gettysburg and made the battlefield a national cemetery to honor the fallen soldiers from both sides. He gave a speech, the Gettysburg Address, that has become one of the most famous in history.

Pickett's Charge, in the Battle of Gettysburg, was a bloody and costly defeat for the Confederacy.

Voices from the Homefront

The war touched the lives of Americans not only on the battlefields. Those at home waited for news of brothers, sons, fathers, and friends. After battles, they gathered outside newspaper and telegraph offices to find out who would or would not be coming home.

In many parts of the country, women and children watched battles being fought in their backyards and villages. Often generals took over homes as a base for their armies.

A teenage girl from Gettysburg recalled the day Confederate troops arrived in her town,

We were having our literary exercises...when the cry reached our ears. Rushing to the door, we beheld a dark, dense mass moving toward town...What a horrible sight! There they were, human beings! Clad almost in rags, covered with dust, riding wildly...

While the men were fighting, women struggled to keep farms, households, and businesses running. They took on jobs as factory workers, laborers, and office clerks.

Young children helped with chores once done by older brothers. Families sewed uniforms and flags, rolled bandages, raised money for the war effort, and wrote letters to the troops.

Women volunteered as nurses and hospital workers. Some disguised themselves as men and went to fight. Sarah Edmonds fought for the Union army as Private Franklin Thompson for two years without being discovered. Other women worked as spies and smugglers on the homefront. Rose Greenhow was a famous Confederate spy.

Women and children were eager to help the war effort.

As the war dragged on, the South suffered from shortages of food, clothing, and other essential items. Southerners managed as best they could, often becoming very creative. Women smuggled medicines across enemy lines hidden under their skirts. They made clothes out of old curtains and flour sacks. They drank coffee made from ground acorns.

But for many the situation became so bad that family members wrote to their soldiers begging them to **desert**. Toward the end of the war, many southern soldiers did desert.

One wife wrote,

My dear Edward–I have always been proud of you, and since your connection with the Confederate army I have been prouder of you than ever before. I would not have you do anything wrong for the world, but...Edward, unless you come home, we must die.

Many southern women had a difficult time surviving while their husbands were off fighting the war.

Early in 1864, the Union army, with far more troops, arms, and supplies, advanced on the Confederate forces. In August General William Tecumseh Sherman captured the city of Atlanta, Georgia.

He marched his army from Atlanta to the Atlantic Ocean, destroying everything in his path. Those trapped in the path lost homes, farms, and towns. Many packed their belongings and fled ahead of the army.

A 10-year-old girl under siege in Atlanta wrote in her diary,

We can hear the cannons and muskets but the shells we dread. One has busted under the dining room table which frightened us very much. One passed through the smokehouse and a piece hit the top of the house. We stay very close in the cellar when they are shelling.

With Atlanta in ruins, General Sherman's army made preparations to leave the city and continue its "march to the sea."

Voices from the Underground

Long before the Civil War, people were fighting to abolish slavery. One of the first great abolitionist leaders was William Lloyd Garrison.

Free African Americans joined the movement as well. Powerful spokespeople such as Frederick Douglass, an escaped slave from Maryland, and Sojourner Truth, a freed slave from New York, convinced Northerners that slavery was wrong. Many abolitionists, including some Southerners, actively helped slaves escape from the South by operating the **Underground Railroad.**

In 1831 William Lloyd Garrison published a newspaper called *The Liberator*, which became the voice of the abolitionist movement.

Sojourner Truth helped support the work of the Underground Railroad. In the years following the war, she fought for women's rights.

The Underground Railroad was a network of escape routes from the slave states to the free states and Canada. It got its name because of the secret way it worked. A network of people provided food, directions, and safe hiding places to escaping slaves. The hiding places were known as stations, and the guides were called conductors.

Levi Coffin and his Quaker family lived at the crossroads of three major escape routes in Indiana. They helped more than 3,000 slaves escape.

Harriet Tubman was an escaped slave who made the journey back to the South no fewer than 19 times to guide others to freedom.

Levi Coffin made this log entry:

...the fugitives sometimes came to our door frightened and panting... having fled in such haste and fear that they had no time to bring any clothing except what they had on...

Harriet Tubman became a famous conductor on the Underground Railroad, whose escape routes are shown on this map.

Information about escape routes was passed from slave to slave through songs and word of mouth. The escaping slaves often traveled on foot. They traveled at night and hid during the day in "safe" houses. Special signals, such as a quilt on a clothesline or a candle in a window, let them know which houses were safe.

It was a crime to help escaping slaves. The slaves faced capture by sheriffs, slave catchers, and lynch mobs. Slave owners offered rewards for the capture of their slaves.

When the Civil War broke out, the abolitionists hoped President Lincoln would **emancipate** (ee-MAN-suh-payt) the slaves.

This painting, called "A Ride for Liberty—The Fugitive Slaves," was painted by Eastman Johnson. It depicts a black family fleeing to freedom. Johnson based the painting on a battle he had witnessed.

But Lincoln feared that if he freed the slaves right away, it would divide the North. The slave-owning states still loyal to the Union might secede.

On January 1, 1863, Lincoln issued the final Emancipation Proclamation, which declared that all slaves in the areas held by the Confederacy were free. However, it did not include slaves in states loyal to the Union or in territory the Union had retaken.

Abolitionists hailed the Emancipation Proclamation as a triumph of a moral right.

The Emancipation Proclamation also allowed African Americans to join the Union army. At the start of the war, they had been turned away by the army. Many worked as spies, cooks, nurses, and laborers, but they were not allowed to be soldiers. Now more than 180,000 joined up to fight on the Union side.

Many people believed that African Americans would not make good soldiers. But they soon proved their courage and ability. By the end of the war, African Americans had won 23 medals for bravery and had fought in nearly 500 battles. Sergeant William Carney was the first African American to be awarded the Medal of Honor.

Make Connections

Have you ever been discriminated against? How did it make you feel?

African-American soldiers were eager to fight for the Union cause.

Voices of Leadership:
FREDERICK DOUGLASS

Frederick Douglass was a leading voice for African Americans before and during the Civil War period. From the moment war broke out, he urged Lincoln to free the slaves and allow black troops to fight. He believed these actions would strengthen the North and weaken the South.

Douglass saw the war as a path to freedom for all African Americans. After Lincoln issued the Emancipation Proclamation, Douglass helped recruit African Americans for the army. Many former slaves joined. Douglass worked to get them equal pay and treatment. He persuaded Lincoln to use them in combat. African-American soldiers quickly earned the respect of many and helped the North win the war.

Once let the black man get upon his person, the brass letters, U.S., let him get an eagle on his button, and a musket on his shoulder and bullets in his pocket, and there is no power on earth which can deny that he has earned the right to citizenship.

Frederick Douglass

25

ABRAHAM LINCOLN

Abraham Lincoln, the 16th president of the United States, led the nation during one of its most difficult times. He was a skillful, patient, and firm leader.

Lincoln argued against slavery, claiming that it "was a moral, a social, and a political wrong." But his first loyalty was to the Union. He was determined to fight for his vision of the nation's future.

Despite initial battle losses, weak generals, and frequent disagreements within his own government, Lincoln accomplished his goal. When the time was right, he freed the slaves. Lincoln supported the 13th Amendment to the Constitution, which was passed by Congress in January 1865. It ended slavery throughout the nation. Lincoln died in April 1865, eight months before the 13th Amendment became law.

[W]e here highly resolve that these dead shall not have died in vain—that this nation, under God, shall have a new birth of freedom— and that government of the people, by the people, for the people, shall not perish from the earth.

Abraham Lincoln, The Gettysburg Address, November 19, 1863

JEFFERSON DAVIS

Jefferson Davis was the only president of the Confederate States of America. Davis believed strongly in states' rights. When he took control of the breakaway government, he said that the people of the Confederate states wished only "to preserve our own rights and promote our own welfare."

Davis had trouble getting the various Southern states to work toward a common cause. He also was stubborn and refused to accept advice. Although the South had excellent military leaders, he did not always listen to them. But Davis's strong will kept the Confederate war effort going for four long years despite the power and resources of the North.

[W]e feel that our cause is just and holy; we protest solemnly in the face of mankind that we desire peace at any sacrifice save that of honour and independence...all we ask is to be let alone; that those who never held power over us shall not now attempt our subjugation by arms.

Jefferson Davis, April 29, 1861

27

ULYSSES S. GRANT AND ROBERT E. LEE

Ulysses S. Grant was a decisive general. In early 1864 he was appointed commander of all Northern armies. He led the crushing attack on the South, cornering General Lee and forcing his surrender at the town of Appomattox Court House, Virginia, on April 9, 1865.

Grant wrote later of the surrender, "I felt like anything rather than rejoicing at the downfall of a foe who had fought so long and valiantly."

Robert E. Lee was against secession and slavery. But his first loyalty was to his home state, Virginia.

Lee was the greatest military leader of the war. Under his leadership, Confederate forces won many battles. But they could not hold out against Grant's assault. After the surrender, Lee told his troops, "Men, we have fought through the war together. I have done my best for you. My heart is too full to say more."

Ulysses S. Grant

Robert E. Lee

A House Reunited

> *With malice toward none; with charity for all; with firmness in the right as God gives us to see the right, let us strive on to finish the work we are in; to bind up the nation's wounds; to care for him who shall have borne the battle, and for his widow, and his orphan to so all which may achieve and cherish a just and lasting peace among ourselves, and with all nations.*
>
> Abraham Lincoln, Second Inaugural Address, March 4, 1865

The war ended in 1865. More than 620,000 soldiers lost their lives. Many towns, cities, farms, factories, and railroads in the South were destroyed. The South's economy had to be rebuilt.

Sadly, Lincoln never lived to see the North and South reunited. On April 14, 1865, five days after the war ended, he was assassinated by John Wilkes Booth.

Columbia, South Carolina, lies in ruins after its fall to the Union forces of General William Tecumseh Sherman.

The end of the war marked the end of more than 200 years of slavery in North America. However, true freedom and equality for African Americans was still not a reality. They had fought for their freedom in the Civil War; now they had to fight for the right to equal citizenship.

Although difficult times lay ahead, a new and stronger nation was to emerge from the war.

No more shall the war-cry sever,

Or the winding rivers be red;

They banish our anger forever

When they laurel the graves
  of our dead!

Under the sod and the dew,

Waiting the judgement day:

Love and tears for the Blue,

Tears and love for the Gray.

(Stanza 7, "The Blue and the Gray," by Francis Miles Finch)

Point

Reread

Skim the book in order to identify primary source documents. How do the words from those who lived through that time period help you better understand the experience of the Civil War?

These gravestones, decorated with Memorial Day flags, mark the resting places of Union soldiers who died at Camp Sumter.

Glossary

abolitionist   (ab-uh-LIHSH-uhn-ihst) a person who worked to end slavery in the United States (page 3)

desert   (duh-SERT) to leave military service without permission and not return (page 18)

emancipate   (ee-MAN-suh-payt) to free from slavery (page 22)

fife   (FIGHF) a small, high-pitched flute (page 11)

popular sovereignty   (PAHP-yoo-ler SAHV-ren-tee) a decision process whereby the people of each state could decide by popular vote whether to permit slavery in their state (page 4)

secede   (suh-SEED) to formally withdraw from a union (page 5)

Underground Railroad   (UHN-der-GROWND RAYL-rohd) a system of escape routes run by an informal network of people working secretly to help slaves escape (page 20)

Index